SCOOBY-DOO'S

LAUGH-OUT-LOUD

JOKES!

by Michael Dahl
illustrated by Scott Jeralds

STARRING...

SCOOBY-DOO!

Shaggy! Velma!

Fred! Daphne!

...AND MORE!

Published by Curious Fox, an imprint of Capstone Global Library Limited, 7 Pilgrim Street, London, EC4V 6LB – Registered company number: 6695582

www.curious-fox.com

CAPG34346

Original illustrations © Hanna-Barbera 2015
Illustrated by Scott Jeralds

ISBN 978-1-78202-241-1 (paperback)
18 17 16 15 14
10 9 8 7 6 5 4 3 2 1

A CIP catalogue for this book is available from the British Library.

SET LIST:

SCOOBY-DOO!

ANIMAL JOKES!

What time is it when you see six chickens outside?
Easy, it's six a-cluck!

What happened when the cow ran into the barbed wire fence?
***Udder* destruction!**

When did the pony answer the teacher's questions?

Whinny had to!

What did the horse say when it fell?
"Help! I can't giddy-up!"

How does a cowboy keep track of his cattle?
He uses a cow-culator!

Why did the sheepdog keep walking along the road?
It didn't see the ewe turn!

Who is a chicken's favourite composer?
Bach! Bach! Bach!

What do you call a really cold cow?
An Eski-moo!

Who's the cow with the sunglasses
and the drumsticks?

He's a moosician.

Where do cows go if they're tired of eating grass?
A calf-ateria!

Where do most horses live?
In a *neigh*-bourhood!

What did the chickens do when they lost the football match?
They cried fowl!

Why do cows lie down in the rain?

To keep each udder dry.

What do you call the hair on a cow's upper lip?
A moostache.

A pig, a cow and a chicken held up a bank. How did they get caught?

The pig squealed!

Why did the calf cross the road?
To get to the udder side!

Have you heard about the farmer who thought he was a goat?

He'd felt that way ever since he was a kid!

How did the sick pig get to the hospital?
In the ham-bulance.

Why do chicken farmers do so well at school?

They're always egg-selling!

How do you know when it's time for the cows to go to sleep?

When it's *pasture* bedtime.

Have you heard about the farmer who needed more room for his pigs?

He built a sty-scraper!

Have you heard about the farmer who drove his cows on a bumpy road?

He wanted a milk shake!

Have you heard about the farmer who crossed a cow with an octopus?

He got an animal that milked itself!

I don't think this cow has any milk.
Well, try the udder one!

Do you know that scientists think they have discovered bones on the Moon?

Jinkies! Sounds like the cow didn't make it!

18

How did the lobster cross the sea?
It moved from tide to tide.

Have you heard about the man who thought he was
an electric eel?
It was shocking!

Where do dolphins come from?
Finland.

Why do sharks swim in salt water?
Because pepper makes them sneeze!

What do you call photos of a piranha?
Tooth-pics!

When do ducks wake up?
At the *quack* of dawn!

VELMA: Did you know that whales are very musical creatures?

SHAGGY: Really? I suppose that's why they play in orca-stras!

What's the best time to buy canaries?
When they're going "cheep"!

Have you heard about the duck who didn't go "Quack" but went "Moo" instead?
Sounds as though it was learning a "moo" language.

Where does a squid keep its wallet?
In an octopurse.

What did the snail sitting on top of the turtle say?

"Slow doooownn!!!!!"

What do you call a duck that eats gunpowder?
A firequacker!

What do you get if you cross Cinderella with a fish?
Glass flippers!

What do you call a bird that's out of breath?
A puffin.

What kind of bird will steal soap from the bath?
A robber duck!

Where does an octopus like to relax?

In an arm-arm-arm-arm-arm-arm-arm-arm chair!

MAN'S BEST FRIEND (AND OTHER PETS)

24

What kind of dog loves bubble baths?
A shampoodle!

Where do bunnies go if they're sick?
The hop-ital.

What do you call a cheerful bunny?
A hop-timist!

Why did the bunny stop jumping?
It was un-hoppy.

Have you heard about the mother cat that swallowed a ball of wool?
Yeah, she had mittens!

Where do cat lovers go on holiday?
Purrrr-u!

Why did the rabbit go to the bank?
It needed to *burrow* some money!

VELMA: What's Shaggy doing out in the garden with a shovel?

FRED: Cleaning up the Scooby-Doo-doo!

FRED: What do you call little dogs that like to visit the library, Scoob?

SCOOBY: Uh, hush puppies?

Why did the rabbit go to the barber?
It was having a bad hare day!

What do you get if you cross a frog and a dog?
A croaker spaniel!

What did Scooby say when he
sat on sandpaper?

Ruff!

... a fish with no eyes?
Fsh.

... a bear with no ears?
B.

... a fly without wings?
A walk.

... a bird on an aeroplane?
Lazy.

... a lamb with no legs or head?
A jumper!

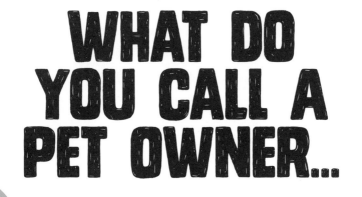

... who has scratches all over his face?
Claude.

... who carries her pet tortoise wherever she goes?
Shelly.

... whose dog always makes holes in the garden?
Doug.

... who loves to touch all the animals in the
pet shop?
Pat.

... who keeps bees?
Buzz.

... whose pet camel doesn't have any humps?
Humphrey.

... who put his right hand in a lion's mouth?
Lefty!

34

How do you scare away bugs?
Call a SWAT team!

What do termites do when they want to relax?
They take a coffee table break!

How do fleas travel from dog to dog?
They itch-hike!

What does the queen bee do when she burps?
She issues a royal pardon!

What insect flies, drinks blood and talks in code?
A Morse-quito!

Why was the firefly sad?
Because her kids weren't very bright!

What did one flea say to the other?
"Shall we walk or take the dog?"

Name the fastest insect in the world.
The quicket!

How many insects does it take to fill a flat?

Ten ants!

What did the termite say when he walked into the saloon?

"Is the bar tender here?"

What do little bees like to chew?
Bumble gum.

What's a mosquito's favourite sport?
Skin-diving!

What are just-married spiders called?
Newly webs!

What did the mother worm say to her son when he came home late?

"Where in earth have you been?"

What happened when Scooby chased the monkey
with a stick of dynamite?
It went BABOOM!

What kind of bear is always wet?
A drizzly bear!

Have you heard the joke about the skunk trapped in
the Mystery Machine?
Never mind. It stinks.

Why was the frog sent home from school?
It was hopper-active!

What did Shaggy say to Fred when they were hiding from the tyrannosaurus rex?
"Doyouthinkhesaurus?"

How do elks send messages to each other?
Moose code.

What's Scooby's favourite snack at the zoo?
Chocolate chimp cookies!

Why do you never see a camel
in the jungle?
**Because they're so
good at camel-flage!**

What language do polar bears speak?
North Polish.

What happened when the chameleon walked over the feather?
It was tickled pink!

Why did the monkey always wear shoes?
So he didn't have bear feet!

Why did the leopard wear a stripy jumper?

So it wouldn't get spotted!

Why did the crocodile cough?
It had a frog in its throat!

What do you call monkeys that are best friends?
Prime-mates!

Why aren't elephants very good dancers?
Because they have two left feet.

What is a llama's favourite drink?
Llama-nade!

What is big, muddy, has tough skin, and can put people into a trance?
A hypno-potamus!

What is a polar bear's favourite meal?
Ice bergers.

What kind of clothes do kangaroos wear?
Jumpsuits!

What kind of shoes do frogs wear?
Open toad!

What do you call a baby hippo that still
wears nappies?
A hippo-potty-mess!

What do you call a lion that eats your mum's sister?
An aunt-eater!

Which snakes are the best at maths?
Adders.

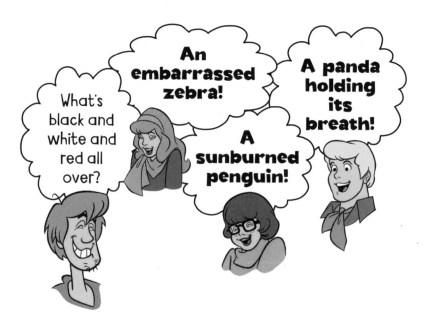

What is big and grey and grey and grey and grey?

An elephant stuck in a revolving door.

What do you call a gorilla that has bananas
growing out of each ear?

**Anything you want.
It can't hear you!**

How do rabbits go on holiday?

By hare-o-plane!

What is a python's favourite game?
Swallow the leader!

Is it hard to spot a leopard?
No, they come that way.

What kind of music do bunnies like?
Hip-hop!

What does a mother snake do if her baby
snake has a cold?
Viper nose!

Do you know
how to make an
elephant stew?

Yep. Just
keep it
waiting for
an hour!

How many skunks fit in the Mystery Machine?

Quite a phew!

What did the boa constrictor say to the monkey?
"I've got a *crush* on you!"

Scientists have discovered the bones of a prehistoric pig.
They're calling it Jurassic Pork!

What do you call a cobra with no clothes on?
Snaked!

What did one toad say to the other?
"Warts new with you?"

What do you call a baby kangaroo that stays indoors?

A *pouch* potato!

What's light and fluffy and swings from trees?
A meringue-utan!

What do you get if you cross an alligator with a bank robber?

A crook-odile!

What did the judge say to the skunk?
"Odour in the court!"

I hate going outside when it's raining cats and dogs.

Don't worry, as long as it doesn't reindeer!

What did the leopard say after dinner?
"That sure hit the spots!"

What did the scale say when the elephant tried to step on it?
"No weigh!"

What kind of animal has white fur, lives in the North Pole and likes to ride horses?
A polo bear!

What do you give an elephant that feels sick?

Plenty of room!

What did the nut say when she sneezed?
"Cashew!"

What did the spaghetti say when it got tangled up?
"Knot again!"

What did the tomato say to
the bacon?
**"Lettuce get
together soon!"**

What did one steak knife say to the other?
"You look sharp!"

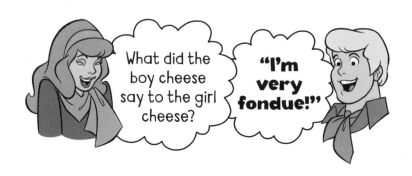

What did one plate say
to the other plate?
"Dinner's on me!"

What did the orange peel say
to the orange?
"I gotcha covered!"

What did the cheese wheel say when he crossed
the finish line?

"I'm so Gouda at this!"

What did the mother tomato say to the baby tomato
behind her?

"Come on, ketchup!"

CUSTOMER: Excuse me, waiter, but will my pizza be long?
WAITER: No, sir, it will be round.

Have you heard about the neutron that went to the restaurant and ordered a pizza?

"How much do I owe you?" asked the neutron.

The waiter said, **"For you? No charge."**

Why don't you ever see a snail queuing up at a drive-through restaurant?
Because they don't like *fast* food!

What did the richest man in the world make for dinner every night?
Table reservations.

Why was the restaurant chef arrested?

Because he was beating the eggs and whipping the cream!

Cooks run in my family.

They should!

Why was the customer so angry with the Italian restaurant?

I don't know, but she certainly gave the waiter a pizza her mind!

CUSTOMER: Sir, why is my food so messy?

WAITER: You told me to *step on it*!

What did the zombie order for lunch?

Pizza, with everyone on it!

NUTRITIOUS KNEE-SLAPPERS

Why did Scooby smear raspberries all over the road?
To go with the traffic jam!

How do you know that carrots are good for your eyes?
Well, have you ever seen a rabbit wearing glasses?

How do you unlock a banana?
With a mon-key!

What does a confused hen lay?
Scrambled eggs!

What kind of nuts do you eat in outer space?
Astronuts.

Why did the orange stop in the middle of the road?

It ran out of juice.

Why did Little Miss Muffet push Humpty Dumpty
off the wall?
He got in her whey.

What happens when a banana gets sunburned?

It peels!

If I had five apples in one hand and six oranges in the other, what would I have?

Really big hands!

What do you call the best pupil at corn school?
The "A" corn!

Why did the woman divorce the grape?
She was tired of raisin' kids!

Why did the tomato turn red?
It saw the salad dressing!

How do you make an artichoke?
Grab it by the throat!

What's red, round and has a sore throat?
A hoarse radish!

Why were the raspberries so sad?
Because their mum was in a jam!

Like, Velma, why did you give the teacher a PC?

Because the shop was all out of Apples!

Shaggy, why are you staring so hard at that carton of orange juice?

Because it says, "Concentrate."

Why did the cabbage win the race?
Because it was *a head!*

What's the difference between a guitar and a fish sandwich?
You can't tuna fish sandwich!

Why were the apples thrown off of Noah's Ark?
Only pears were allowed!

Have you heard the joke about the peanut butter?
I better not tell you. You might
spread it!

Which fruit is always teasing the others?

The banana-na-
na-naaaa!

BELLY LAUGHS FOR BREAKFAST

What do mermaids spread on their toast?
Mermalade.

Where do horses eat their morning cereal?
At the breakfast stable!

How does Darth Vader like his toast?
On the dark side!

What's the best way to guarantee breakfast in bed?
Sleep in the kitchen!

What's red, wiggles and flies through the air?
A jellycopter.

What did the computer do for breakfast?
It had a byte to eat.

What did the cup say to the tea bag?
"You're in hot water now!"

Why was the cook so unhappy about working in the margarine factory?
She was hoping for something butter!

Why didn't the teddy bear eat his lunch?
He was stuffed!

Why do seagulls fly over the sea?
**If they flew over the bay,
they'd be bagels!**

I taught Scooby not to beg at the table.

How did you do that?

I let him taste my cooking!

FAVOURITE SCOOBY SNACKS

What do you get when you mix an aardvark
with a pizza?
Ant-chovies!

What's a dog's favourite pizza?
PUParonni!

What do you get when you mix a golfer with
flour, sugar, butter and cocoa powder?
Chocolate putting!

Why do asteroids taste better than chicken
sandwiches?
Because they're meteor!

What do little dogs eat at
the cinema?
Pupcorn.

What do you get when you mix a cow, a chicken, and a loaf of bread?
A roost beef sandwich!

What do you get when you mix a centipede with a chicken?
Drumsticks for a month!

What do you get when you mix a snake with a basket of apples?
A pie-thon!

What did the grape say when the elephant stepped on it?
Nothing. It just gave a little wine.

What amount of salt can hurt?
A pinch.

Where does Scooby buy his food?
At the SUPERmarket!

What do balloons like to drink?
POP!

What does Shaggy serve, but Scooby never eat?
A tennis ball.

What do you call a pretend penne?
An impasta!

I feel like spaghetti tonight.

That's funny, you don't *look* like spaghetti!

Why are frogs always so happy?
They eat whatever bugs them!

Why do watermelons have
fancy weddings?
**Because they
can't elope!**

FOOD KNOCK, KNOCKS

Knock, knock!
Who's there?
Figs.
Figs who?
Figs the doorbell. It's broken!

Knock, knock!
Who's there?
Olive.
Olive who?
Olive here. Why are you in my house?!

Knock, knock!
Who's there?
Orange juice.
Orange juice who?
Orange juice coming outside to play?

Knock, knock!
Who's there?
Dishes.
Dishes who?
Dishes me. Who are you?

Knock, knock!
Who's there?
Bean.
Bean who?
Bean a while since I last saw you!

Knock, knock!
Who's there?
Lettuce.
Lettuce who?
Lettuce in. We're cold!

Knock, knock!
Who's there?
Doughnut.
Doughnut who?
**Doughnut ask.
It's a secret.**

DELICIOUS DESSERTS

Why did Shaggy eat his maths homework?
Because his teacher said it was a piece of cake.

What's white, has a horn and gives us something nice to eat?
The ice cream van!

Why did the biscuit go to the doctor?
He was feeling a little crumby.

How do you make a milk shake?
Take it to see a scary film!

Why did the baker stop making doughnuts?
She was tired of the hole business.

What does chocolate do when it hears a good joke?
It snickers.

What kind of dessert roams the Arctic tundra?
Chocolate moose!

Why did Scooby go to the doctor after
eating the cupcakes?
Because he got frostingbite.

What kind of
keys does
Shaggy always
carry?

Cookies!

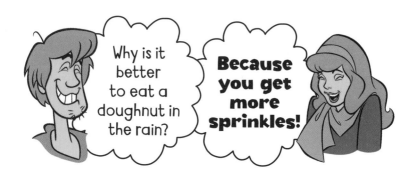

Why is it better to eat a doughnut in the rain?

Because you get more sprinkles!

CHILD: How much for a taste of the gingerbread?
WITCH: Don't worry. It's on the house!

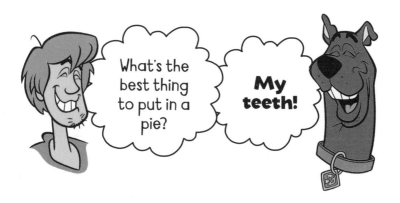

What's the best thing to put in a pie?

My teeth!

How do the Mystery gang make biscuits?
With Scooby-dough!

Why don't they serve chocolate in prisons?
Because if the prisoners eat too much, some of them might break out!

What's big and white and lives on Mars?

A Martian-mallow?

CUSTOMER: Do you have ice cream on the menu today?
WAITER: No, I wiped it off.

Who can serve ice cream faster
than a speeding bullet?
Scooperman!

What's a maths teacher's favourite dessert?
Pi.

What grows in the treetops and likes to eat chocolate?
A cocoa-nut.

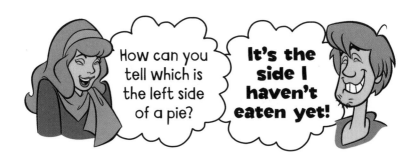

Why did the student work at the bakery?
Because she *kneaded* the dough!

MORE FOOD FUNNIES

What do you call cheese that is sad?
Blue cheese!

What did the microwave dinner say after it was packaged?
"Oh no – foiled again!"

I feel full!

How full?

AW-ful!

What happened to the caveman who saw a sheep
struck by lightning?
He invented the baa-becue!

Why is it difficult to starve on a beach?
**Because of all of the
sand which is there!**

Why did the doctor give mustard to Scooby
when he had a fever?
**Mustard is the best thing for
a hot dog!**

What do you call a pig who's just recovered from a cold?
A cured ham!

What does a pirate like on his salad?
Thousand Island dressing!

How can you tell if a clock is hungry?
It always goes back four seconds.

Why is six afraid of seven?
Because seven eight nine!

Why couldn't the sesame seed stop gambling?
Because she was on a roll!

SCOOBY:
When can we have something to eat?
**ASTRONAUT:
At launch time!**

Where were the first chickens fried?
In Greece!

What's the world's heaviest soup?
Won-ton soup!

What kind of cup is impossible to drink out of?
A hiccup!

I've heard that polar bears like
Mexican food.
**Yeah, especially
brrr-itos!**

What did the police do with the
beefburger?
They grilled it!

What do whales eat for lunch?
Peanut blubber sandwiches!

What do you give a poorly lemon?
Lemon aid!

Which is the best day of the week to eat chicken on?

Fryday!

What kind of lunch do you get when a chicken sits on the roof?
Egg rolls!

Which cheese is made backwards?
Edam.

Why did the light bulb get bigger and bigger?
He kept eating watts and watts!

How do seals make pancakes?
With their flippers!

What do you call cheese that
isn't yours?
Nacho cheese!

What do you get if you cross a duck with a cow?
Milk and quackers!

Where did the spaghetti go to dance?
The meat ball!

Scoob, why isn't your
salad joke in this book?

It was
tossed!

SCOOBY-DOO!

MONSTER JOKES!

What's the best way to help a starving zombie?
Give him a hand!

When do zombies go to sleep?
Only when they're dead tired.

What do zombies like to
eat when they go out
to a restaurant?

The waiters!

Where's the safest place in your
house to hide from zombies?
The *living* room, of course.

What does Godzilla call skateboarders?

Meals on wheels!

Why is Godzilla so good at sneaking up on people?
He's a crept-ile.

What did Godzilla say when he saw a train full of passengers?
"Chew-chew!"

What's the best way to call Godzilla?
Long distance!

Why did Godzilla eat all the furniture in the hotel room?
He had a suite tooth!

Did you hear that Godzilla was sick?
Yeah, it's all over town!

What do you call Godzilla
in a phone box?

Stuck!

How does Dracula like his coffee?
De-coffin-ated!

When did Dracula realize that sunlight could destroy him?

When it finally *dawned* on him!

What kind of dog does Dracula have?
A bloodhound!

Why won't anyone kiss Dracula?
He has *bat* breath!

Why was the vampire studying all night long?
She was getting ready for her blood test!

What do you say to a vampire who wants to go on a date?
"Fangs, but no fangs!"

Why don't vampires have many friends?

They're such pains in the neck!

What's a vampire's favourite fruit?
Neck-tarines.

Why did the zombie lose the card game?
He had a rotten hand!

What do you call a zombie
door-to-door salesman?

A dead-ringer!

What happened when the zombie was late for the dinner party?

They gave him the cold shoulder.

What do you call a teenage zombie with no legs?

Grounded.

What did the zombie do when she lost her hand?

She went to the *secondhand* shop!

What did the little zombie make of his new friends at school?

A pie!

What did the zombie eat after the dentist pulled out all his teeth?

The dentist!

Don't make a vampire angry. **They have very *bat* tempers!**

What does Dracula take when he has a cold?
Coffin medicine!

What do goblins like to put on their toast?
Scream cheese!

That vampire certainly is popular.

Yeah, she has a big fang club.

How did the vampire cure his sore throat?
He spent all day gargoyling!

What do little vampires eat for lunch?
Alpha-bat soup.

Where does Dracula keep his money?
In a blood bank.

Why don't vampires ever race each other?
They're always neck and neck!

Wow! I heard that Dracula knocked someone out with one punch!

ROW! He was out for the Count!

Did you know there's a vampire duck?
Of course. It's Count Quackula!

Why did the vampire fail her art exam?
She could only *draw blood!*

I heard the new restaurant has a vampire for a chef.
Yes, he's Count Spatula!

What do you get if you cross the Mystery Machine with a bloodsucker?

A van-pire!

What do you call a ghost's mum and dad?
Trans-parents!

What do you call a ghost that haunts chickens?
A poultry-geist!

What keeps a ghost cool in the summer?
A scare conditioner.

What did the ghost wear to the dinner party?
A boo tie!

In what position do ghosts sleep?
Horror-zontal!

Where do ghosts go for treats?
The I-scream parlour!

Where do phantoms post their letters?
A ghost office!

What do you say to a ghost when you meet one?
"How do you boo?"

What do baby ghosts wear on their feet?
Boo-ties!

Did you hear that
Dr Frankenstein combined a
cocker spaniel, a poodle
and a ghost?

Yep, he ended up with a cocker-poodle-boo!

What do teenage ghosts wear?
Boo jeans.

What's the first thing ghosts do when they get into a car?
Put on their sheet belts!

Why are ghosts so bad at telling lies?
You can always see right through them.

How do ghosts like their eggs cooked?
Terror-fried!

Why do ghosts take the lift?
It raises their spirits!

What happened to
the mad scientist who
crossed a pig with a
grizzly bear?

**He got a
teddy boar!**

What happened to
the mad scientist who
crossed a UFO with a
wizard?

**He got a
flying sorcerer!**

What happened to
the mad scientist who
crossed a slab of cheese
with Frankenstein?

**He got a really
scary Muenster!**

What happened to the mad scientist who crossed a snake with some building blocks?

He got a boa constructor!

What happened to the mad scientist who crossed a turtle with a porcupine?

He got a slowpoke.

What happened to the mad scientist who crossed a toad with a distant galaxy?

He got star warts!

What happened to
the mad scientist who
crossed a bear cub with
a skunk?

**He got Winnie
the Phew!**

What happened to
the mad scientist who
crossed a newborn
snake with
a trampoline?

**He got a
bouncing
baby boa!**

What happened to
the mad scientist who
crossed an alligator
with a rabbit?

**He had to get
a new rabbit!**

Why didn't the skeleton go to the school disco?
He had no *body* to go with!

Why was the skeleton so afraid of heights?
She just didn't have the guts!

Why did the skeleton keep his head in the freezer?
I suppose he was a numbskull!

Why didn't the skeleton eat the canteen food?
He didn't have the stomach for it.

Where do skeletons go on holiday?
The Dead Sea!

Where can you always find a cemetery?
In the dead centre of town.

What did the film director say when she had finished
her mummy film?
"That's a wrap!"

The doctor told the mummy he had the heart of a
much younger man.
**Yes, and the doctor told him he had
to give it back, too!**

Did you know that skeletons love riding motorbikes?
Yep, they're *bone* to be wild!

What do skeletons order when they go to a restaurant?
Spare ribs!

What did the skeleton dad say
to his son when he stayed in
bed all day?

"Lazy bones!"

Why doesn't the mummy have any friends?
She's too *wrapped up* in herself!

What did the ghost say to his girlfriend?
"I really dig you!"

What does a skeleton say before every meal?
"Bone appétit!"

Who won the skeleton beauty contest?
No body!

Cemeteries are having difficulty finding room for all their guests.

Yes, it's a *grave* problem!

Why did Frankenstein go to the psychiatrist?
He thought he had a screw loose!

Why did Frankenstein go to the restaurant
with a raisin?
He couldn't find a date!

What's Frankenstein's favourite pudding?
I scream!!!

Do you know where Frankenstein lives?
Yes, at a dead end.

I heard that Dr Frankenstein is really funny.
Yeah, he always keeps you in *stitches*!

Why is Dr Frankenstein so popular?

He's very good at making friends.

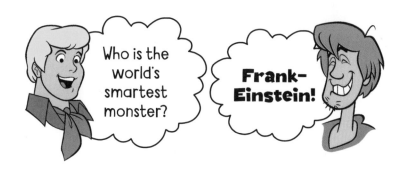

How does Frankenstein eat his lunch?
He bolts it down!

What does it say on Frankenstein's gravestone?
"Rest in Pieces."

How did Frankenstein get rid of his headache?
He put his head through a window and the pane just disappeared!

What did Frankenstein say to the screwdriver?
"Daddy!"

What do you call witches who live in the same room?
Broom-mates!

What do you call a nervous witch?
A twitch!

Watch out! We're being chased by twin sorceresses!
I know! I can't tell witch is witch!

Why was the witch late for the party?
Her broom overswept.

What did the sorceress have for a snack?

A sand-witch!

How does a wizard tell the time?
With a witch-watch!

What do you get when you cross a witch's cat with a lemon?
A sourpuss.

Did you know that witches fall from the sky?
Yeah, and the angry ones fly off the handle!

What happened to the wizard who was badly behaved at school?

He got ex-*spelled*!

What kind of sorceress is always helpful in the dark?

A lights-witch!

What happened when the giant brick monster escaped from prison?

They set up a road block!

What happened when the Human Fly
escaped from prison?
They brought in a SWAT team!

What happened when the cyclops escaped
from prison?
The police had to keep an eye open!

What happened when the evil
hairdresser escaped from prison?

Police had to comb
the area!

What happened when the mutant corn monster escaped from prison?

They called out the cobs!

What happened when a gang of monsters escaped through the sewers?

The police said it was a grime wave!

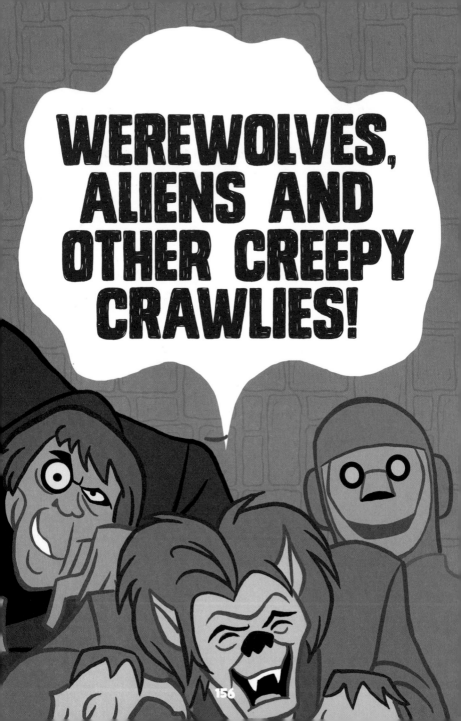

Why didn't the monster ever go out with his friends after school?

He wasn't allowed to play with his food!

How many parents does a werewolf have?

Five. One ma and four paws.

What does a techie pirate wear?

An iPatch.

What should you do if you're attacked by a gang of clowns?

Go for the juggler!

Where did the alien leave her UFO?

At a parking meteor.

What monster eats the fastest?
A goblin!

What planet did the evil aliens crash land on?
Splaturn!

What technique do aliens use for fighting?
Martian arts!

Why do dragons sleep during the day?
So they can fight knights!

Who's the centre of attention at a monster disco?
The boogie man!

Which hand should you use to stroke King Kong?

Someone else's!

How can you tell if there's a monster under your bed?
Your nose touches the ceiling!

What did Godzilla say after he caused
an earthquake?
"Sorry, my fault!"

What do sea monsters like to eat?
Fish and ships!

Why did the headless horseman go to university?
He wanted to get *a head* in life!

Why did the monster's gran knit him a new sock?
She heard that he'd grown another foot!

How do you mend a broken jack-o'-lantern?
With a pumpkin patch!

Why did King Kong climb the Empire State Building?

He was too big to use the stairs!

What do you call a one-eyed monster on a motorbike?
A cycle-ops!

How can I contact the
Loch Ness monster?

Drop it a line!

Why is a cemetery a great place to write a book?
It's full of plots!

Where does the yeti keep its money?
In a snow bank.

What would you say if you saw two cyclopes in a dark alley?
"Eye, eye!"

Did you hear about the monster who was a
Star Trek fan?
**He had one right ear, one left ear,
and one final front-ear!**

Why are ghost children so happy at the end of the week?
It's Fright Day!

What happened when the vampire bit into the cake?
She got frostingbite!

What do ghosts use to wash their hair?
Sham-boo.

Why did the scarecrow win the Nobel Prize?
He was outstanding in his field!

Who is the scariest singer on the planet?
The Grim Rapper.

What's a monster's favourite play?

Romeo and Ghouliet!

Why did it take so long for Godzilla to gobble up Big Ben?
It was time-consuming!

What do you call a hairy monster flying a helicopter?
A whirr-wolf!

Why did the zombie get a massage?
She was a little stiff!

SHAGGY: Poor Scooby! The police put him in prison after he ran away from the slime monster.
FRED: Why?
SHAGGY: **He was arrested for leaving the scene of the grime!**

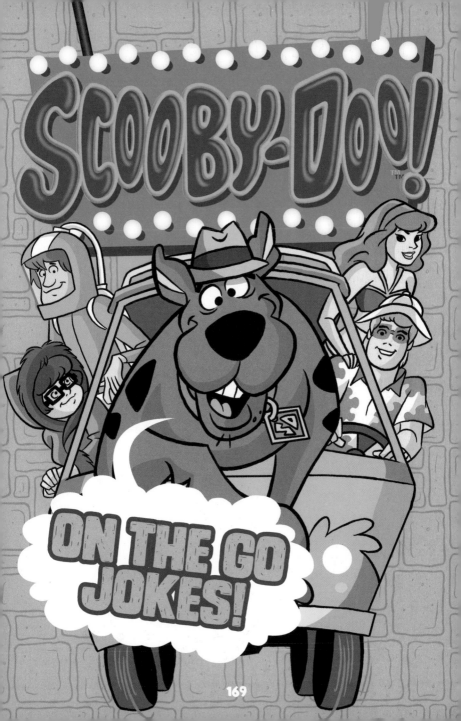

What do you call a city where there are no people?
Electri City.

Which is the cleverest country in the world?
Albania. It has three A's and one B!

Which European country has the least gravity?
No-weigh!

Why did the book go to the psychiatrist?
It kept talking to its shelf!

What do you call a snowman in Spain?
Water.

I hear Scooby might go to university.
Yes, he's been given a dog *collar*ship!

What is the coldest country in the world?
Chile.

LITTLE GIRL: I'd like to buy a plane ticket for Erwood.
TRAVEL AGENT: Erwood? Sorry, never heard of that. Where is Erwood?
LITTLE GIRL: He's over there. He's my brother.

Sorry, I can't go to the dance. I've sprained my ankle.
That's a *lame* excuse!

What do you call a giraffe at the North Pole?

Lost.

What stays in one corner but travels
around the world?
A stamp!

What do you call a fear of the North Pole?
Santa Claus-trophobia.

HIT THE GROUND RUNNING

What should you always drink before a race?
Running water!

Have you heard about the runner who was afraid of hurdles?
He got over it.

Why did they throw Cinderella off of the netball team?
She kept running away from the ball!

Marathon runners can race for miles, and they only have to move **two feet!**

Why is the Mystery Inc. gang always so tired on the 1st of April?

Because they have just finished a march of 31 days!

A sloth went out for a walk and was mugged by a gang of snails. When he reported it to the police, the officer asked, "Can you describe the snails that attacked you?"

The sloth said, **"Sorry, it all happened so fast!"**

What does the winner of a race lose?
Her breath.

Have you heard about the two silkworms who had a race?
It ended in a tie.

What do you call little rivers in Egypt?
Juve-niles.

What happened when a red ship crashed
into a blue ship?
The crew was *marooned!*

Why do ferries have so many
angry people on board?
Because the boat makes them cross!

Where is the English Channel?
**I don't know. My TV doesn't
pick it up!**

What kind of stories are all about boats?
Ferry tales!

How do surfers greet each other?
They wave!

How do surfers clean themselves?
They wash up on shore!

What did Shaggy say to his friend while they were surfing?
"Scooby-Dude!"

Why are pirates called pirates?
Because they arrrrrrr!

Shaggy went to the beach and sat down next to a sunbathing pig. Shaggy said, "It sure is hot." The pig said, **"You got that right. I'm bacon!"**

Is that boat expensive?
No, it's a sale-ing boat.

Where do you find *micro*waves?
On tiny little beaches!

How did the dentist cross the harbour?
He took the Tooth Ferry!

What's the best day to go to the beach?
Sun-day!

How did the penguin cross the glacier?
He went with the floe.

Do you know where to find the Dead Sea?
Dead? I didn't even know it was ill!

188

What has four wheels and flies?
A dustbin lorry!

Why are you so late for school today?
The road sign outside says, "School ahead. Go slow."

What did Dorothy do when her dog got stuck on the yellow brick road?
She called the Toto truck!

Why did the cannibal drive on the motorway?
He heard the service stations were serving lorry drivers!

I don't think you should ever put a goldfish in a tank.

Everyone knows that fish can't drive!

What driver doesn't need a driving license?
A screwdriver!

Why don't you see the Mystery Machine parked outside football matches?
It's not a big sports van.

Have you heard about the magician who was driving
down the road?
He turned into a driveway.

What's worse than raining cats and dogs?
Hailing taxis!

Why does an ambulance always have two medical experts on board?
Because they're a pair-a-medics.

What does a doctor take when she's feeling run down?
The registration number of the car that's just hit her!

What happens when a frog parks in a no-parking zone?
It gets toad away!

What kind of vehicle does a mad scientist drive?
A loco-motive!

How does a puppy carry luggage?
Easy, its little tail is a wagon.

Have you heard about the mechanic who slept under the car?

Yeah, he woke up *oily* the next morning.

When does a van stop working?
When it's re-tyred.

What do you call a laughing motorcycle?
A Yamahahaha!

What do you get when dinosaurs crash their cars?
Tyrannosaurus wrecks!

When does a van go to sleep?
When it's tyred.

Which snakes are found on cars?

Windscreen vipers!

Who has a job driving customers away?
A taxi driver.

Have you heard the joke about the dustbin lorry?
Don't worry. It's a load of rubbish.

Why did the Mystery Machine get a puncture?
There was a fork in the road!

What month do soldiers hate the most?
March!

What do you get when you cross a cowboy
with a map-maker?
A cow-tographer!

What lies on the ground, 100 feet in the air?
A dead centipede.

Shopping is good for helping you see the future!
It helps you see what's in store.

Have you heard about the big game hunter who married the telephone operator?

Their lion is always busy!

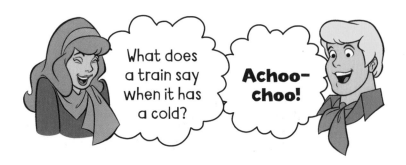

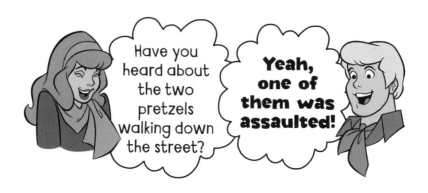

How do trains hear?
Through their engine-ears!

What's the difference between a teacher and a train conductor?
One trains the mind, and the other minds the train.

What is the difference between a well-dressed man on a tricycle and a poorly dressed man on a bicycle?
A-tyre!

CHILD: Doctor, my dog thinks he's an elevator!
DOCTOR: Then send him up to see me.
CHILD: I can't. He doesn't stop at this floor!

How do fleas travel from place to place?
They itch-hike!

Shaggy, why do you have two hair-curlers and two butter knives at the table?

I thought I'd make some roller-blades!

Why is it good to always travel with a barber?
They know all the short cuts!

Have you heard that Scooby fell into an upholstery machine?
Don't worry, he's fully re-covered!

Have you heard about the fire at the circus?
The heat was in tents!

Why can't the train play music?
It's on the wrong track.

I love staying at the hotel.

If you love it so much, why don't you Marriott?

What's the hardest part of skydiving?
The ground.

Why could the vulture only take two
dead badgers with him on the plane?
**Because they were
considered *carrion* items.**

What only starts to work after it's fired?
A rocket!

Why did the police officer arrest
the balloon?
**It broke the law
of gravity.**

What happens when you throw a clock in the air?
Time's up!

Scooby wondered why the
boomerang kept getting bigger...
**...then it finally
hit him!**

What do you get if you cross a dog and an aeroplane?
A jet setter!

Where do locksmiths go on holiday?
The Florida Keys.

Where do buffalo go on holiday?
Rome.

Where do sharks go on holiday?
Finland.

Where do bacteria go on holiday?
Germany.

Where do lumps of sugar go on holiday?
Sweeten!

Where do knots go on holiday?
Tie-land.

Why did the boxer have an awful holiday?
All he packed was a punch!

Where did the worm go on holiday?
The Big Apple.

What do you call a piece of paper that
doesn't go anywhere?
Stationary stationery.

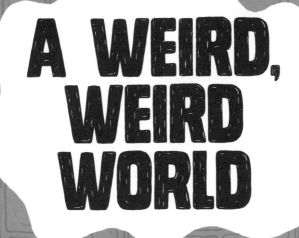

Which is the world's laziest mountain?
Everest.

Which is the thirstiest body of water in the world?
The Gulp of Mexico!

Where can you find the Great Plains?
At great airports!

Which is the fastest country in the world?
Russia.

Why is the Equator boiling mad?
Because it's 360 degrees!

Which statue stands in New York,
holds a torch and sneezes?
**The *Atchoo!* of
Liberty.**

What's a light year?
**The same as a normal year, but
with fewer calories.**

Which is the wettest country
in the world?

The United Kingdom.
The queen has
reigned for
over 60 years!

What did one escalator say to the other?
"I think I'm *coming down* with something."

What did the rucksack say to the hat?
"You go on ahead, I'll go on back."

What did the cowboy say after he was thrown off his horse?
"I've fallen and I can't giddy-up!"

What did the tornado say to the sports car?
"Want to go for a spin?"

What did the jack say to the car?
"Can I give you a lift?"

What did one traffic light say to the other traffic light?
"Don't look! I'm changing!"

What do you say to a cow that walks in front of
your car?
"Mooo-ve over!"

What did the sleeping bag say to the Scout?
"I've got you covered!"

What did the toadstool say when it moved into its
new house?
"Not mushroom in here!"

What did one volcano say to the other?
"I lava you!"

What do you say to a frog who needs a lift?
"Hop in!"

HOW TO TELL JOKES!

1. KNOW the joke

Make sure you remember the whole joke before you tell it. This sounds obvious, but most of us know someone who says, "Oh, this is so funny..." Then, when they tell the joke, they can't remember the end. And that's the whole point of a joke – its punchline.

2. SPEAK CLEARLY

Don't mumble; don't speak too quickly or too slowly. Just speak like you normally do. You don't have to use a different voice or accent or sound like someone else. (UNLESS that's part of the joke!)

3. LOOK at your audience

Good eye contact with your listeners will grab their attention.

4. DON'T WORRY about gestures or how to stand or sit when you tell your joke. Remember, telling a joke is basically talking.

5. DON'T LAUGH at your own joke

Yeah, yeah, I know some comedians crack up while they're acting in a sketch or telling a story, but the best rule to follow is not to laugh. If you start to laugh, you might lose the rhythm of your joke or stop yourself from telling the joke clearly. Let your audience laugh. That's their job. Your job is to be the funny one.

6. THE PUNCHLINE is the most important part of the joke

It's the climax, the reward, the main event. A good joke can sound even better if you pause for just a second or two before you deliver the punchline. That tiny pause will make your audience mentally sit up and hold their breath, eager to hear what's coming next.

7. The SETUP is the second most important part of a joke

That's basically everything you say before you get to the punchline. And that's why you need to be as clear as you can (see 2 above) so that when you finally reach the punchline, it makes sense!

8. YOU CAN GET FUNNIER

It's easy. Watch other comedians. Listen to other people tell a joke or story. Go and see a good comedy show or film. You can pick up some skills simply by seeing how others get their comedy across. You will absorb it! And soon it will come naturally.

9. Last, but not least, telling a joke is all about TIMING

That means not only getting the biggest impact for your joke, waiting for the right time, giving that extra pause before the punchline — but it also means knowing when NOT to tell a joke. When you're among friends, you can tell when they'd like to hear something funny. But in an unfamiliar setting, get a "sense of the room" first. Are people having a good time? Or is it a more serious event? A joke has the most funny power when it's told in the right setting.

How is **Michael Dahl** like a cemetery salesman?

They both like a good plot!

Dahl has come up with more than two hundred good plots, in the form of books, for young readers. He is the author of *The Everything Kids' Joke Book*, *Laff-O-Tronic Joke Books*, the scintillating *Duck Goes Potty*, and two humorous mystery series: Finnegan Zwake (a "wisecracking riot" according to the *Chicago Tribune*) and Hocus Pocus Hotel. He toured the country with an improv troupe and began his auspicious comic career in fifth grade when his stand-up routine made his music teacher laugh so hard she fell off her chair. She is not available for comment.

How is **Scott Jeralds** like a bumblebee hitting a doorbell?

They're both humdingers!

Jeralds has worked in animation for companies including Marvel Studios, Hanna-Barbera Studios, M.G.M. Animation, Warner Bros., and Porchlight Entertainment. Scott has worked on TV series such as *The Flintstones*, *Yogi Bear*, *Scooby-Doo*, *The Jetsons*, *Krypto the Superdog*, *Tom and Jerry*, *The Pink Panther*, *Superman*, *Secret Saturdays*, and he directed the cartoon series *Freakazoid*, for which he earned an Emmy Award. In addition, Scott has designed cartoon-related merchandise, licensing art, and artwork for several comic and children's book publications.